2017. And we find oursel\
Political turbulence. A
£200m while tower block. _ _ _ _ _ _ _ _ _ _
in flammable materials to save a few thousand. The
leadership of a world power falling into the hands of
a man who tweets his policies in the small hours with
the emotional coherence of a teenager after one too
many Jägerbombs and a dodgy kebab. Extreme
weather. Poet Tony Walsh showing the power of words
and humanity after the Manchester bombing, and
Heather Heyer's mom doing it after Charlottesville.

Meanwhile, people are doing what they've always done.
Hustling. Getting by. Laughing, loving, mourning, and
looking after each other. Dreaming of better times.

Into the midst of all this, I'm casting this book of
poems out upon the waters, to travel where it will. My
thoughts on the world we live in, in all its tawdriness
and its jaw-dropping beauty. I hope you enjoy them,
and this fine fine planet we call our home.

cheers

Steve

'I first met Steve when he was playing flute in a punk-hippy band in Leeds. He wasn't a great flute player, but he was always a poet. Always quick with a quip and up for an argument. But lately his words have somehow multiplied and exploded, his storytelling sharpened, his ideas tumbling over themselves to be heard.

If you've seen these poems read out you'll know Steve knows how to tell 'em – most of them are best heard live. But there's a gorgeously chatty, slangy, informal tone running through these written poems. *Here, mate, listen to this. Honestly, it's true. I swear. Lean in closer.*'

Boff Whalley, musician, authot, playwright.

'Some books of poetry make you wonder why they were written. Not this one. These poems throb with life – muscular, passionate, emotional, rational, compassionate. These poems are the verbal equivalent of earworms. These poems *had* to be written.'

Brenda Read-Brown, poet.

'This is indeed a fine, fine collection. Human and humane. Incisive and at times acerbic. There is here poetry that bites with 'sharp perfect teeth', but there is also laughter, joy and hope. Pottinger is a master of his craft and a truly coherent voice for our times.'

Emma Purshouse, poet.

'Steve Pottinger is a POET with a capital everything. See his poet's feet, set fast in Midlands concrete. See his long poet's arms, reaching out to draw close to his heart life's done-in, done-down and done-over. See his whopping great poet's fists, full of love and rage, ready as needs be to caress or deck humanity in all its beautiful stupidity. And hear him, as comfortable painting to life the drunken nighthawks of the last train home as he is tearing into those who'd judge *a child's laughter / a mother's hope / or a girl's dreams / by which side of a border they live on.*'

Jonny Fluffypunk, poet.

'A poetic story-teller of great skill, Steve weaves comical tales of last-train-chaos with defiant paeans to England, the West Midlands in particular.
With pathos and grace, he creates collages of the everyday – mixing our collective vulnerability and humanity with stone-cold contempt for the powerful and the immoral.'

Laura Taylor, poet/performer

'Steve's poems are bostin. They're like a comforting arm on your shoulder, while the other hand pinches you into submission.'

Spoz, poet.

At 66 000 miles per hour
we're barrelling through space
on this blue-green ball of love and guns
it's a fine fine place.
Strap in, enjoy the ride, and feel
the wind upon your face.

a

fine

fine

place

steve pottinger

ISBN: 978-0-9932044-3-2

typeset by Steve at Ignite.
www.ignitebooks.co.uk

Printed and bound in the UK
by Bell & Bain Ltd,
Glasgow.

'The world is a fine place and worth fighting for'
Ernest Hemingway

'We are monkeys with money and guns'
Tom Waits

'It's just a ride'
Bill Hicks

Contents

The poem **Stabberjocky**
was previously published in the anthology
'Poems for Jeremy Corbyn'.

Videos of the following poems
can be found on Youtube:

Every night, the same dream
Broadcast
A single step

The last train out of Birmingham on a Saturday night.

this train is full
of the drunk and the befuddled
the sozzled and bedraggled
the misplaced and the pure puddled
and it's rolling through the night
late-shift workers and young dancers
ravers chemically enhanced
shady blaggers, shifty chancers
who are higher than a kite

someone asks *'Is this train for Wolverhampton?'*
the answer? *'No, it's bound for Mars'*
and I think *I knew I should have*
had a piss at New Street
but hey, you can't knock a £2.40 return
for space travel when it comes to value

these carriages are full
of girls in glad-rags and thick make-up
a lad who just won't wake up
who, two stops back, said he'd take up
any offer of a fight
drunk as lords and talking codshit
wearing Guinness hats and tight-fit
stonewashed jeans or nylon sports kit

we travel at the speed of light
(in the Birmingham area this is about 50-60mph)

and the woman from Ghana
lays her head on her husband's shoulder
and falls asleep, smiling

we fly past motorways and pylons
estates of sodium lights and sirens
canals of sticklebacks and silence
as deep and black as ink
and the lads are getting plastered
as the drinking games get faster
two are nasty bastards
and the third's a missing link

but we are on the 23.39 to outer space
and we fear

nothing

this carriage is a blur
of fake tans and thigh-high hemlines
late-night burgers mixed with red wine
flirtatious banter and come-on signs
and the world of broken dreams
is left behind, forgotten
we're drinking champagne from the bottle
it's a party at full throttle

but you know nothing's what it seems
because then, without warning,
the train stops
spits us out into the middle of
wherethefuckarewe?

and now we're stumbling and mumbling
tottering and tumbling
our confidence is crumbling
we're blinking and we're lost
the thin dry air of some new planet
is this Mars? or just North Thanet?
stuff this, I can't stay here, man it –
how much will a taxi cost?

we queue to go from here
to a better place
and in the conga line of comedowns
I see the woman from Ghana
and she's still smiling

Every night, the same dream

the stink of diesel and of fear which
everyone's pretending is not here
because if they do not name it, it will not be real
but in the hot bodies of the strangers pressed
around her she can feel
the tension of a panic only held at bay
like sea-sickness, with iron will, good fortune,
muttered prayers
inshallahinjesusnameinshallahinjesusname
they rise and fall, jaws clench and clench again
she is one of hundreds, women, children, men
crowded together, huddled, packed tight in
each has just room to breathe
a space no bigger than a coffin
and something is wrong she knows it
feels the rising terror
with each lurch of the trawler
she knows this was an error, a mistake
a wrong turning that was made
when all other roads were blocked
and the price that must be paid
won't be measured out in crumpled dollar notes
but in the treasure of her hope
and then the boat
tips a little someone screams
water swills around her ankles

there is a scramble
for the hatch and those who can
kick and punch and fight their way out
but she is going down
blowing bubbles of her dreams
and even as she drowns
she tells herself
she paid her money someone must save her
she paid her money someone must save her
she paid her money someone must save

and Katie wakes in bed
salt water on her tongue
the smell of death around her
wonders what she has done wrong.

Humanity

I was standing in line
at check-in
at the bakers
queuing for the morning bus
for water
in the hope of a job

I was buying flowers for my love
drinking coffee
smoking a cigarette
wondering where the next meal
would come from

I was going to tell the boss to stick it
smiling at the memory of you
feeling the sun on my face
wishing blessings on the day

when

the bomb dropped
the car exploded
he blew himself up
the truck drove into the soldiers
and the sky fell in

then all was choking dust and silence
the sound of someone screaming

and it was him
and it was her
and it was them
and it was me

and it was you.

How to get everything you ever wanted

1.
Invent a war.
Something bloody and fratricidal.
Lose an uncle to barrel bombs
a brother to secret police.

2.
Three years in, flee.
Pack only what you can carry:
clothes, smartphone, children, cash.
Slip away at night, in silence.

3.
Take your leave of the flat, bakery, office,
rubble-filled streets where the kids once ran
shell of the cafe where old men
drank *qahwa*, played *sheesh beesh*.

4.
Cross a border to camps, to life on hold.
Everyone knows someone who's gone
before them, dreaming of better.
Here there is only the absence of war.
It's not enough.

5.
Moving is what you do.
Railway tracks, verges, fields.
Rest in olive groves, wake in orchards.
One foot in front of the other
over and over and over.

6.
The world is cold-eyed border guards
sandwiches and blankets.
You never know what is coming.
One day, open hand. Another, fist.

7.
You learn the words you need
in a new language.
Arbeit. Ja. Nein. Thank you. Please.
The smile that shows you know to be grateful.

8.
Evenings you sit at the kitchen table
talk to friends in cities far away
about places that have gone
about old men who drank *qahwa*
played *sheesh beesh*.

9.
At night you dream of rubble, and of home.

Bullring

I fell in love with you, Birmingham
when you started knocking things down
strode into the new century
with a glint in your eye
levelled flyovers and circuses to rubble
put the shopping centre in your sights
spat on your hands, and set at it.

As each floor fell, and you opened up the sky
with jackhammers, diggers, and machines
I smiled. It felt like saying goodbye
to a maze of misplaced hopes, a catalogue of errors
to subways, disappointments, stunted trees
and crippled bloody pigeons.
On days when the sun shone
the air smelt of new beginnings.

Breezeblocks and steel, girders, concrete beams
trundled away, truckload by truckload, revealed
an empty hillside I never knew was there
and then you dug down, and in my wildest dreams
I never expected this. Concealed
beneath the brickdust, excavated and laid bare
a bed of rich red stone, a sudden wonder.
We paused on our way past to gawp
and have a gander.

You're still the same, Brum.
Streets of buskers and the press of shoppers
workers, traders, barrow boys and rogues
preachers who promise hellfire and salvation
amidst the chat of Urdu and Somali,
patois, Pashto, Farsi
Polish, midland vowels, and Irish brogues
a city of a thousand trades
now singing in a hundred tongues,
always changing.

And those of us who saw that day
behind the hi-vis and the hard hats
this glowing rock, an ever-constant earth
the colour of love, fire, joy,
of blood and birth
we know, we will bear witness
that what lies beneath our feet

felt a lot like forgiveness.

England

Straight off the bat let me say
I was never a fan
I mean don't speak ill and all that
but if we're clearing the decks
wiping the slate clean
getting it all out in the open
then....
you were bloody hard work, England,
not easy to live with, let alone love.

You see, you kept making me and my friends
sit cricket tests I was never going to pass
took our taxes and our labour
but still left us feeling second class
because our roots stretched back
to other cultures, other shores
and other teams made our guilty, secret hearts
beat a little faster, race a little more.
Even now, it's like you can't help yourself
some scoundrel starts waving the flag
critical thought goes out of the window
and next thing you know
you've tanked yourself up on bigotry and lager
giving it '2 world wars and 1 world cup'
like you fired the winning shot yourself.
I mean really, England? Really?

I've seen you running for the bus
in the mornings, and it's not pretty.
You're a heart attack waiting to happen
hypertension, clogged arteries, dodgy knees
it's all history, for fuck's sake
do yourself a favour, let it go.

And you were the chink of fine china
the tyranny of manners and the old school tie
tut-tut-tutting about the enemy within
turning a blind eye while someone
did your dirty work
gratuitous truncheons
battles in beanfields
cover-ups and never-challenged lies.
So, like I say, it wasn't the best of starts.
I had to leave to learn to love you
get far enough away to see both sides
of the coins in your pocketful of shrapnel
find the fist that read *'love'*
not just the one that promised *'hate'*.

And out there,
on the other side of the world
I found I missed you
missed your dirt under my fingernails
hankered after your way with words
your dirty laugh
your seaside postcard humour

and your beautiful mongrel language.
Every time you open your mouth
history tumbles from your lips
in dialect and accent
a pulsing archaeology of trade
invasion, conquest, immigration
the ebb and flow of populations
making room making homes
and getting assimilated
learning there's precious few of life's problems
not cut down to size with another cup of tea
and a couple of biccies.

You're not dead.
You're just evolving
re-inventing yourself
getting your nails done
putting on your glad rags
for a night out on the town
and I will find you
on top of the moors
quoting Benny Hill and Shakespeare
feasting on samosas and flagons of cider
slapping the taut drum of your stomach
where it spills over the waistband of your trousers
– *all paid for, kid!* –
proud as punch
Falstaff, as I live and breathe
paddling in the shallows

beyond the deckchairs and the donkeys
giggling in Gujerati
the hem of your sari trailing in the cold North Sea
salty and wet while your wide-eyed kids
play shoot-em-up in the arcades
mither you for fish and chips
support City and United
and ride the bus home
with their heads full of dreams
knowing love triumphs
over cricket tests every time
and their hearts beat
proud and strong.

Stabberjocky
(with apologies to Lewis Carroll)

'Twas Brexit, and the slithy Gove
did frottercrutch in dwarfish glee;
he snicker-snacked the Camerove,
Machiavelliadastardly.

Beware the stabberjock, my son!
The empty eyes, the robo-glint!
who fellobrates the Murdocrone
the Ruperturtle übergimp!

He pallerised the BoJo cloon
they chummed upon their sunderbus
emblazoned it with fibberoons
and bambulluntruthoozled us.

The tousled toddler slaughterchopped,
his destiplans an Eton mess,
the slubbergubby gollumgove
a shadowhand of viciousness.

O gipperchund! And vomberblast!
The skitterchit of slick and sly
the snicker-snack of backstablades
the scrabblage to ruthlerise.

The bubberchut of charismissed
the turdletruck of banalbore
is patterfrondled on the head
a pawn upon a checkerboard.

Beware the stabberjock, my son!
The empty eyes, the robo-glint!
who fellobrates the Murdocrone
the Ruperturtle übergimp.

Moving on

wave goodbye to solidarity,
xenophobia's in vogue
jackboots are just so passé,
let's vote for stylish brogues
who needs angry demagogues?
we're a pair of raffish rogues
the cheeky charming chancers
we've moved on

we used to hate the blacks and irish,
now it's albanians and poles
we've learned to use the glottal stop,
and patronise the proles
and we've privatised the contract for the bloke
who digs the holes
deeper deeper deeper
we've moved on

don't try and set events in context,
the past is best forgotten
the system works to our advantage,
while we tell you that it's rotten
we blame the foreigners, the unemployed,
the poor folk at the bottom
does that all sound a bit familiar?
let's move on

the power that dropped into our hands,
we didn't quite expect it
the siren songs of sovereignty
has led us all to brexit
by the time you get your country back,
there's every chance we will have wrecked it
and while you're picking up the pieces
we'll move on

a simple slogan in a complex world,
we want our country back
the fist that masquerades as bumbling
is still a weapon that attacks
a foolish flag-wrapped falsehood
flying in the face of facts
you'd think by now we should know better

moving on

Broadcast

This is a party political broadcast
on behalf of the moon on a stick party.
We promise you a moon. On a stick.
You. And you. And you. And you. And you.
Let us be clear.
There will be moons on sticks for all
each and every one of you
bigger moons, better moons
moons to make Britain great
sticks to warm your cockles.
A moon on a stick for every hard-working family
for schoolkids for pensioners
two moons per household, minimum
moons that work at weekends, nights, holidays
sticks available on a strictly monitored 24-7 basis
moons that rise to the strains of
Land of Hope and Glory
moons to be the envy of the world
efficient moons, productive moons
moons emblazoned with the union flag
moons in red white blue, blue white red
any combination you want
moons the colour of sovereignty
moons to end fifty years of hurt
optimistic moons, happy moons
moons with perfect teeth and white smiles

with bigger dicks, pert breasts, and tangle-free hair
eager moons, compliant moons
moons that never say no
moons for heroes
moons that are loving it
moons that go better with coke
moons that *oh yes*
moons because you're worth it
moons that put you in control
finger lickin moons that go *va-va-voom*
don't read the small print
just sign on the dotted line.

Let us be clear
we're all in this together
in it for moons.

We promise you moons.

Failing that
there will always be the stick.

In Which The Tory Election Strategy Is Found On The Back Of A Fag Packet Stained With Lynton Crosby's Tears.

Make her the Vera Lynn of kitten heels
with the flag framed in soft focus
while cameras ignore or airbrush out
the casualties and corpses.

Bang on about strength and stability
and keep your fingers crossed
if the voters see through this charade,
we've lost.

Haiku: An Interim Report On The Re-training Of The Current Leader Of The Conservative Party In Preparation For Her New Role Later This Autumn.

Not bad, Theresa.
Now just once more, with feeling:
You want that with fries?

Comrade Osborne and
the Little Red Book

The chancellor's autumn statement
and McDonnell's quoting Mao!
It's a joke. A jest. A jolly jape
to illustrate just how
George is selling off our assets
to global profiteers
and the Chinese state is buying up
the things which we hold dear
while the media says... nothing
a conspiracy of silence
on illiterate economics
and structural state violence
against the vulnerable and needy
the sick, the weak, the poor
while under Georgie-boy's agenda
those who have will get still more.

So, a quote from Mao. It's theatre.
Or is it thoughtcrime? Watch the spin
from a free press owned by powerful men
who say the sky is falling in
and the world is surely ending
and the only thing it took
was to point at a pantomime villain
and quote from Chairman Mao's little red book.

Because the Mail has wet its knickers
The Sun's gone apoplectic
they see the thin end of a fat red wedge
of Marxist dialectic.
There's communists in Westminster!
The left are going loony!
Corbyn causes cancer!
He's a Trotskyist! A Moonie!
He hates you and your children!
He's dangerous, and weird!
If Labour get their hands on power
they'll make you all grow beards
and call your children Karl and Castro,
Leon, Che, and Vladimir,
while your hope dies in collectives
and your lives are lived in fear!

Hysteria and hyperbole
employed with one sole aim
to solidify the status quo
fix the rules, and rig the game
while the ground is sold beneath our feet
our future swept away
and airstrip one is put in hock
while capital makes hay.
And when your children ask *Who did this?*
And when? And why? And how?
remember the chancellor's autumn statement
and McDonnell, quoting Mao.

Poem For A Royal Correspondent On The Occasion Of The 90th Birthday Of Mrs Saxe-Coburg Gotha

it was a time we thought would never come
unbelievable, and then some
after all those years of playing dumb
Nicholas Witchell went feral

there was consternation at the BBC
dowagers spluttered in cups of tea
when out of the blue, precipitously
Nicholas Witchell went feral

if you saw it you'll know what I mean
live on air and at the scene
he said **** the ****ing ******* queen
Nicholas Witchell went feral

he was a viral sensation – no ifs, no buts
hashtag trending *#NicksGoneNuts*
who'd have thought it? that ginger klutz
Nicholas Witchell went feral

he wore a tin hat made of silver foil
said balls to deference, and the royals
was fouler-mouthed than Frankie Boyle
Nicholas Witchell went feral

he dished the dirt and he spilled the beans
on Phil the Greek and Mrs Queen
you wouldn't believe the things he's seen
Nicholas Witchell went feral

he said Liz copped a feel the first time he met her
said it made him feel bad but he's glad that he let her
she's a little old dear who smelt slightly of feta
Nicholas Witchell went feral

he shocked the nation to the core
then the men in white coats burst in through the door
and no-one saw him any more
Nicholas Witchell went feral

but we whisper his name to each other, discreetly
and keep his memory alive in the spray of graffiti
and chuckle to think of that day when – completely –
Nicholas Witchell went feral

Ne'er the twain...

The President a dyed buffoon
a giant all butt and belly
a genius a toddler
who thinks he channels Machiavelli
bestrides a brave new world it's bullshit
where truth is destined for the axe
the winner in this tangerine dystopia

#alternative facts

A single step

one day soon
after due consideration
of all the available material
newspaper reports, history, the facts
after casting the bones of lost *mojados*
against the ghost of a threat of a wall
reading the tea leaves and the runes
seeing how the cards fall
and pawing through the entrails
of a freshly-despatched lentil bake

and with each of these confirming
what I already know to be true
which is to say
that the famously sculpted hairstyle
can only be a very public cry for help
I'm going to write Donald J Trump a letter
and offer him sanctuary in the West Midlands

because everyone deserves a second chance
somewhere they can start again
and we're tearing down paradise
slab by concrete slab
letting the nibbler eat our past
so we move forward
into something bigger, better, bolder

a future woven from steel and dreams
and yeah, maybe we'll get it wrong
at least we're trying

and I will show him motorway junctions
constructed entirely from pasta
markets which bustle with every shade of skin
fruit piled high and vegetables to die for
a city centre echoing to the sound of violin
accordion, double bass and trumpet
as the buskers fill the canyons of New St
with melody, rhythm, and joy
playing ragtime jazz like it grew
out of the badlands of Bucharest
and belongs here too

I'll point out to him that music has no borders
while we feast on samosas, scratchings, and kormas
and when the girls walk by
on their way home or off to college
in crop-tops, sports gear, hijabs, and tight jeans
and Donald watches and can't help himself
and says something mean
one of them will tell him in no uncertain terms
that what they choose to wear
and do with their bodies
whether they love boys or girls or boys
is no-one's business but their own
You got that, bab?

and I'll chuckle into my coffee
let Donald chomp down on his chip butty
chew on that

and we will take a bus out of the city
with a driver who's from Krakow or from Cradley
passengers from Lagos and from Lye
and walk along the towpath by the freight lines
underneath the big Black Country sky
and talk
and when we've finished talking
in the wasteland where the furnaces once stood
we'll bury all his hatred
unremembered and unwanted
stamp the earth down hard and know
that this is good

and then, the important stuff
we'll go and get him a haircut

and later that evening after three pints of ale
when the sour lemon of his tight pursed mouth
finally breaks into a smile
and Donald beams like the good-natured bloke
he'd forgotten he could be
I'm going to go for broke
invite Katie Hopkins over
let the two of them loose on Broad St
on a saturday night

it'll be carnage

they'll be hell for leather at the two-for-one
dancing to '80s anthems
singing along to Abba songs
remembering what it felt like to be sixteen
feeling the beat from the tambourine
spilling out of the club and into the night
staggering through the city on just the right side
of a skinful, grabbing a 2am kebab
yes to chili sauce! throw on those jalapenos!
and somewhere halfway down Hurst St
with showtunes ringing in their ears
when the boa-waving drag queen
plants a sequinned kiss on his cheek
and Donald blushes and grins
as Katie gives his hand a squeeze

right then,
there,
in that moment
the fences round the no-go areas of their minds
will tumble and Donald mumbles
something about our common humanity
surprising himself
the words sound odd in his mouth
so he tries them again for size
as Katie reaches up and kisses him
presses herself against his thighs

and they run through the revellers
out to the back streets of Digbeth
where, up against a crumbling factory wall
they make soft, fumbling, urgent, inadequate love
in the half-light of morning
ignoring the catcalls from passing cars
holding each other tight
knowing there is only this this this
and ah! the world may not be perfect
but it is what it is

sweaty, radiant, unashamed
dishevelled and contented
they catch their breath
tuck themselves back in
laugh at the absurdity of it all
take each other's hand
and saunter off into the sunrise

and I will wake alone that afternoon
the taste of vodka on my tongue
pick up my pen
and write a letter to Vladimir Putin.

These winter days

when the sun
hating the cold dark mornings
hits snooze on the alarm three times
crawls out of bed grumbling
about stiffness in the joints
damp, a bunged-up nose,
is a bear with a sore head
till the coffee kicks in
last of the milk and the motivation

queues at the bus-stop in the rain
with the other heavenly bodies
doesn't get a seat – again –
Mercury chattering on her mobile
about what Mars did
and how he loves her really
wise up, love
everyone knows what the boy's like
anger-management issues
plain as the nose on his face
someone should tell him
sun bites his tongue
it's not worth the aggro

then work, boss, office, drudge
same old same old

and the bus back home
Mercury sobbing in the corner

one day, sun tells himself,
he'll move somewhere better
do that sea, sand, tropical beach thing
Alpha Centauri always goes on about in her letters
but deep down he knows he lacks
the get-up-and-go
and when summer comes
he'll be back down the park with a cold one
lolling about like always
making hay

Missing the point

you

walking past the bushes
eyes only for the screen

fingers skittering on keypad
typing searching typing

joy evoked by the scent
of the first hawthorn blossom
of spring

into your smartphone

#epicfail
#yoursearchreturnednoanswers

Keytown Xmas

is Kevin dressed as Superman
sparking one up at the front door
is frost sparkling in the scrapyard
on the serried battlements of cars
is cheap plastic toys in poundland paper
value vodka and a singalong
is Sharon smiling through the bruises
wondering how it all went wrong
is the factories with shattered windows
machines now inches deep in rust
is the beer cans piled inside the graveyard
full to empty, dust to dust
is piebald ponies on the waste ground
pigeons circling the church where the travellers sing
is christ and salvation and battered transits
and the silent night of no trains running
is kids in the skate park and the smell of ganja
the sparrowhawk that no-one sees
is the dog fox growing fat on take-outs
sunlight tumbling through the trees
is Jamal skinning up in his Fiesta
bass the soundtrack to his haze
is sirens always wailing somewhere
zero-hours and hi-vis days
is hope bought on the never-never
the TV on for background din

sprouts and spuds and jokes and crackers
laughter loud and full and high and thin
is the alarm that rings and rings unanswered
is tinsel blowing down the road
is waiting till the pub is open
money missing money owed
is dreaming of the winning scratchcard
the lottery of luck come good
you tell yourself you couldn't leave
but deep inside you know you would
is the place you're born its roots inside you
friends and kith and kin and more
is walking the dog by the last of the pit bonk
loving and hating and loving it all
is the history of coal and steel
of locks and keys and graft and skill
the thundering ghost of dropping forges
for better for worse for good or ill
is the prayers you make but can't believe in
a drunken carol tattered pride
is too much of one not enough of the other
always the bridesmaid and never the bride

and it's Kevin dressed as Superman
carrying too many pounds to get away with lycra
but not letting that stop him
and he's sparking one up
squinting into the sunshine
sucking the life out of it

taking a deep breath
squaring his shoulders
stepping back inside
and leaving trouble for tomorrow

like super-heroes do

Why you are #beachready

because you deserve to feel
       the sun on your skin
       hot sand between your toes
       to slough off the workday drudge
       and free your smile
because it will be fun
because ice-cream melts fast
       and tastes good
because it's your laugh that matters
because no-one ever died thinking
       the best thing they did
       was spend three years on a diet
       so they could wear a bikini
       for half an hour on the one decent day
       we have in a british summer
       then spend that thirty minutes
       holding their stomach in
       afraid to breathe

       really – do the maths

because you're beautiful – right now
because when did you last build a sandcastle?
because you will return home
       sun-kissed and contented
because you can be certain that

as soon as a cheap hustler
in a bad suit
tries to sell you something
then you don't need it
because there are small fish
scurrying crabs and anemones
in the rock pools
and they don't give a toss
about your curves
your weight
your BMI
because I am a lot like an anemone
and most men are
because at night you can go
skinny-dipping
and it will feel like liberation
because it's not the office
because life is too short to be miserable
because you can gaze out
to where the sea meets the sky
off into the infinite blue
and out there
light years away
on a planet we haven't even found yet
a creature is dipping all seventeen
of its three-foot toes in the water
and gazing back at you
because well it might be, right?
because never let anyone tell you

what you can and cannot do
never let anyone tell you
what you can and cannot do
never let anyone tell you
what you can and cannot do
because your dreams are worth more than gold
and you are your dreams and more
because the best moments in your life
can be stitched with seaweed, shells
the sound of surf
the memory of laughter
sunlight shimmering on water
because I may not know much
but I'm sure of this
because you're beautiful right now
and you're ready
and you want to

go.

Pub poem

here we dreamed, made plans,
drowned sorrows, drank to your memory
found quiet crossword corners
cheered along when City scored
and that afternoon
when we hid from the world
and I told you I love you
no pint in the world
has ever tasted better

snafu

saturday night
and in the budget hotel
on the outskirts of town
we're in the bar

drinking
putting work behind us
the festival the mud
the guitarsdrumsbass
crack of snare
check 1-2 1-2
touch more keys in the vocal mix mate
nice one check check

living the dream
three pints in
and midnight well behind us
7am alarm still hours away
time for one more
and a few more stories, yeah?

when the bottle-blonde
across from us
gets up sashays over
eye contact all the way
slides two cards onto our table

never breaking her stride
is gone

I pick them up, read
high-class escort
best in the north-west
re-evaluate the cheap pink chiffon
off-the-shoulder visible charms
the fella with her
the pair of them
like guests at a wedding
of people they don't know

here in a budget hotel
on the outskirts of town
packed with drunk anonymous men
and she's selling distraction
cheap pink chiffon action
living the dream

I go to bed alone

in the morning
the talk is all of
the incident
one of our guys saying
when he went to bed
she was sparked out in the corridor
copper standing over her

bloke in the doorway of the room
blood on his face
saying she went crazy
drew a knife on him

word is
he'd served in the forces
could handle himself
she picked the wrong one there
jab to the jaw
one shot
incident

situation normal
all fucked-up
no-one asking
about the back story
just a plump lass in chiffon
out cold in a budget hotel
on the outskirts of town
a long way from home

I think how the card said
high-class escort
best in the north-west
and not one of us
remember her name

and then it's back to

1-2 1-2
touch more keys in the vocal mix mate
nice one check check

living the dream
check check

living the dream
check check

living the dream
check check

living the dream

Any resemblance to actual persons, living or dead, is purely co-incidental

we've boosted a car and got the motel room
frozen pizzas, hair dye, wigs, and thrift shop clothes
borrowed a wheelchair
and Photoshopped a fake ID
to turn you into someone no-one knows

we've got friends across the country
in condos, backwoods, cities, and on farms
in schools and universities and ghettos
who'll shelter you and keep you safe from harm

we're ready

and when the Secret Service agent
who has a mother, sister, daughter, lover
who believes in the dream
who knows this will mean a desk job
in the back office of a one-horse town
with no horse for the rest of his days
and who doesn't care

when he looks the wrong way at the right moment
and you exit stage left pursued by no-one
slip into the back seat of a car that turns right
at the lights and is gone

then, Melania, then and only then
as you sit on a motel bed
munching on a slice of margherita
waiting for the dye to take
designer clothes stuffed in a bin-bag by the door
wearing someone else's cast-offs
that pinch and sag, are nowhere near your size,
and the smile your mama taught you
creeps back to light your eyes

then, your life will begin

and when the fat toad in his gilded rage
screams his fury in one hundred and forty
characters of CAP LOCK
and proclamations of revenge

then we will tweet him in our thousands
#ShesNotYours
#ShesNotYours
#ShesNotYours

Fox sake

I can't prove it, of course
when they demand cold facts,
clipboards, scientists in white coats
pointing at graphs, reeling off numbers
setting the issue beyond doubt
with their earnest voices, sensible haircuts, and
specs you only have to look at
to know this is serious, and so

when they tell me my claims count for nothing
without a stack of studies
peer-reviewed under laboratory conditions
a list of recognised authorities
as long as my arm and then some
working parties, references, and charts

when they dust off contracts I'd forgotten
jab at my signature
point at the small print
remind me of
the legal standing of *clause xvii b*
the incontrovertible truth of the footnotes

then what can I do
but shrug my shoulders and grin

because we know
that these last few weeks
the sun has shone more brightly
blossom burst out on long-dead trees
the earth has dipped herself in stardust
and spun giddy through the cosmos
humming snatches of favourite melodies
while we have rollicked and rutted like foxes
wrapped in twisted sheets, our world
a funk of wide-eyed wonder

beneath a harvest and a hunting moon
we are turning back time
with clawmarks and hot breath
loving ourselves immortal
in a den of teeth
and sharp, fierce, loving cries

Swallows

when the swallows arrived
next spring
we were ready

with paperwork, permits, and protocols
with questions and with quotas
forms filled in, in triplicate, by hatchet-faced clerks

with suspicion, without sentiment
and speeches from our government
about the need to keep our country safe
from those from foreign parts

swallows found flying into the country at night
were shipped back to the continent
wings clipped, in chains
citizens with swallows' nests on their property
were fined, named, shamed
if the traffic was bad
or the trains were late
the swallows were blamed

while politicians railed
and there was gloating in the press
our skies were emptier, quieter
our summer less blessed

each morning we were reminded
that we had been saved from
the unspeakable machinations and evils
of swallows

and we taught ourselves to understand
this was for the best

Let me warn you...

...about this poem

this poem is loaded, minted, filthy rich
money squirrelled under offshore mattresses
coming out of its accountants' ears
Croesus in a sharp suit and a car

no surprise
if it's a touch full of itself
a wee bit cocky
got arrogance to burn
best thing since sliced bread
since before sliced bread
since sliced bread was a twinkle
in its daddy's etc.

and it's full of it
the same old schtick
the *man of the people* bullshit
just a regular kind of guy
kind of a poem
that's what it'd have you
believe

it's not a poem like other poems
so make some allowances

cut it some slack

and when one day
this poem hits someone
professors of english literature
will line up round the block
to justify it
explain the role of the right hook
in 21st c verse
and the bardic tradition

while the poem smiles
a neat white smile
of sharp perfect teeth
cold eyes and calculation
and some mother's son
lies bleeding and forgotten
on the floor

yeah

let me warn you about this poem

This will be a re-run

it'll be the comfort of the saturday afternoons
of your childhood
sat in front of the TV with bread and dripping
watching John Wayne set the world to rights
with a gun
it'll be Kenneth More on tin legs reaching for the sky
with a re-mix of stirring music Vaughan Williams
would kill for
it'll be a tearjerker in the final reel
where you know the hero's going to die
but his girl will remember him forever
it'll be you me us being the good guy
rescuing the damsel
putting the planet back on its axis
making sure all is well with the world
popping down the pub for a half a bitter
and a sing song
saving Blighty for another day
it'll be black and white
it'll be clarity
it'll be mom dad fido eternal happiness
everything you could want for a shilling
cowboys and indians
bang bang you're dead
but just till tea-time
beans on toast and final score

the magic of the FA Cup
granddad checking the pools
shaken and not stirred
it'll be bombing Syria by the end of the week
it'll be nothing like Libya
it'll be don't mention Afghanistan
it'll be Iraq again
like we did last summer
it'll be fiction
it'll be make-believe
it'll be tears before bedtime
it'll be bombs not strategy
it'll be innocent victims
it'll be refugees
it'll be bombs bombs bombs
not strategy
it'll be black and white
it'll be clarity
it'll be mom dad fido eternal happiness
it'll be Kenneth More weeping
into his pillow

this will be a re-run

21st c enlightenment blues

Rattling through the low hills
in the darkness and the endless endless rain
this train is overcrowded
because this train is overcrowded
because this train is always overcrowded
and the conductor's now a manager
a voice we never see
mumbling something through the tannoy
about weather and delays.
We used to have seats
now we stand
and this is progress.

Outside
the airwaves are full beyond bursting
with reports of death death death
of young men gorged on bitterness and bullets
who want a world in their own image
who take Kalashnikovs to café bars
and spew their hatred into headlines.
The numbers mount
twenty, forty, eighty
one hundred and twenty-nine
and journalists run to keep up
as our disbelief stumbles beside them
barely able to count

deafened by the online chatter
lost in the conviction of our own powerlessness
to do anything that matters
while the 24-hour news channels
send you numb with repetition
driving home the horror
till you scream at them to
stop

stop

stop

stop

stop

before you too view your neighbour
through the sour veil of suspicion.
You know we trust people less now
than we did twenty years ago
and this is progress.

We've more than enough hate to go round.
Anyone has access to a keypad and a cause
and it's easy to believe that our future
is Paris, Beirut, Baghdad, Nairobi
that hope is so last century
now it's all about circling the wagons
and building the walls
higher higher higher

like the prophets of doom
have always wanted.
They see the end of days in everything.
Here, barbarians at the gate;
there, immorality, apostates.
They go to war over oil
or the meaning of texts
written by desert tribes
trying to make sense of the senseless
forgetting we're idiot monkeys
running over a small blue planet
reliant on rain and the heat of a star
for pretty much everything.
Arguing about skin colour
and nationality like it matters
filling cyberspace with ignorance
and white-hot indignation
judging a child's laughter
a mother's hope
or a girl's dreams
by which side of a border they live on
or the god they follow
while the rest of us scramble
to put food on the table
look after the ones we love
wait for the rain to ease off
or the rains to come
and pray our kids will have a better life
that they'll see progress.

And the voice of the train manager
announces our arrival at a station
mutters an apology for overcrowding
due to breakdowns, floods,
inadequate investment, cancellations
asks us to take all our belongings with us
to take care when disembarking
thanks us for choosing to travel with etc.
He sounds tired and beaten-down
but when he wishes us a safe onward journey
and says he hopes he sees us soon
this evening, for once
I decide to believe him.

If you want more poems, blogs,
and news of what I'm up to,
pop along to the website:

stevepottinger.co.uk

notes on some of the poems in this book

Last train: Best. Journey. Ever. I love the West Mids.

Every night, the same dream: a response to Katie Hopkin's comment 'these migrants are like cockroaches'. You'll find a video of this poem on Youtube.

How to get everything...: because I had enough of people telling me refugees are after our 'generous benefits'.

Bullring: one of an occasional series of love poems to the West Midlands.

England: a response to a question posed by artist Carolyn Bayliss: what would you say at the funeral of England? As someone who grew up proud of his mongrel background, I'm intrigued by the concepts of nationhood and identity and what people take them to mean.

Stabberjocky: a nonsense poem about the nonsense politics that surrounded the Brexit campaign.

Moving on: directed at those politicians who build their careers on pandering to people's prejudice and fear. Nigel Farage, Boris Johnson, I'm looking at you, for starters.

Broadcast: which brings us to this, and a video on Youtube.

Comrade Osborne...: watching the media spin this stunt – directed at a Conservative chancellor and his policies – was an education in deliberate misinformation.

Poem For A Royal Correspondent...: the poor, poor man, destined to spend his career at the BBC enthusing about all things royal. He'll snap one day, mark my words.

A single step: because sometimes you have to dare to dream. And take the piss. Oh, and there's a video of this on Youtube, too. Another love poem to the West Midlands.

Keytown Xmas: this time, a love poem to my home town.

Why you are #beachready: a response to an infamous ad on the London Tube, which featured an impossibly beautiful woman in a bikini and the slogan 'Are you beachready?' I mean, really, who's that help?

snafu: a true story.

Any resemblance...: when Mrs Trump finally makes a break for freedom, remember you read it here first.

Let me warn you...: in no way inspired by an incident where Jeremy Clarkson punched his producer. Absolutely not.

This will be a re-run: for armchair jingoists everywhere.

21st century enlightenment blues: written on a (crowded) train journey two days after the attacks on Paris.
Despite everything, a poem of hope.

I wasn't going to include this poem. The world is awash with broadsides aimed at Mr Trump, and it seemed foolish to pay this ignorant and arrogant man any more attention than is absolutely necessary. Then there was Charlottesville. And his shameful response.

So stuff him. Here's a bonus poem.

If you enjoy it, there's a video on Youtube.
Fill yer boots.

Thoughts on the rise to power of president-elect Donald J Hairstyle.

The marketing can be top notch
the PR team outstanding
they can say this is a big job
they've been proud to have a hand in
but their puffing and their posturing
is pathetically absurd
because everyone knows
you can't polish a turd.

You can give it a makeover
which will dazzle and bewitch
it can be wearing a vajazzle
and have tassles on its tits
it can be hanging off the arm
of some celeb from the telly
but it's a disturbing shade of tangerine
repellent, foul, and smelly
and the media go ga-ga
and repeat its every word
while we shake our heads and mutter
about polish, prats, and turds.

It can insist that it's incredible
The best. It really is.

But when it claims that you'll be great again
it's selling you some shiz.
Engage your other senses
see and smell above the chatter
and recognise behind the bling
the stink of faecal matter
I know experts aren't in vogue right now
but they've all of them concurred
that you're wasting time and effort
when you're polishing a turd.

Drop the kids off. Do the school run.
Give the turtle's head release.
You've been touching cloth for far too long
you've earned a little peace.
Relax, exhale, expel, and void
and flush. You're feeling lighter
refreshed, relieved, reminded
that the future's looking brighter
when you aren't buying into bullshit
like a fantasy Lolita
turning tricks for some fat old bloke
who's excited by excreta
while you tell yourself he loves you
but in case you hadn't heard
it'll end in tears, and they'll be yours
if you're polishing a turd.

Yes, you tell yourself he loves you
but in case you hadn't heard
it'll end in tears, and they'll be yours
when you're polishing a turd.

enjoying the ride?

Ignite Books is a small, independent publisher. This book is the latest in our series which we hope puts thought-provoking, entertaining writing before a new audience. We have a lot of fun doing this, but we also survive on a shoestring budget and a lot of graft. So, if you've enjoyed this book, please tell your friends about us. You can also find us on twitter, so drop by and say hallo. And to learn more about what we do, or to shop for our other publications, you'll find our website at **ignitebooks.co.uk**

Thank you.